Torsten Andreas Hoffmann
New York New York

C Mann
From
Grandma
1/15/05

Blick vom World Trade
Center auf den öst-
lichen Teil von „down-
town" rund um die
Wallstreet

View from World
Trade Center to east
downtown around
the Wallstreet

Vorwort

Nur ein Silberstreif am blanken Himmel. Das Flugzeug wäre unsichtbar, würde sein schlanker Körper nicht das Licht reflektieren. Es gleitet auf die goldene Wetterfahne der steilen Kirchturmspitze von St. Pauls Church Downtown Manhattan zu – und wohl in gehöriger Entfernung vorbei. Erfasst von der Kamera des Fotografen Torsten Andreas Hoffmann im Spätherbst des kriegsträchtigen Jahres 2001. Der Turmhelm über den geschlossenen Schallfenstern im Säulenkranz der aufgelassenen neobarocken Kirche steigt friedlich in die Atmosphäre auf, ein schönes, farblich und formal wunderbar austariertes Bild. Aber die schreckliche Erinnerung ist da, ein Wissen, eine Erfahrung, die den Blick auf Bilder, namentlich die technischen und elektronischen, womöglich nachhaltig und vielleicht für immer verändert hat.

Ein paar Monate zuvor nahm der Fotograf ein Bild mit demselben Motiv auf, aus nahezu der gleichen Perspektive, ebenfalls mit starker Teleoptik, allerdings in Schwarz-Weiß. Ein scheinbar ähnliches Bild und doch völlig anders. Denn auf diesem Bild wäre das Flugzeug gar nicht zu sehen gewesen, wäre verdeckt worden von der bildfüllenden Rasterfassade eines der beiden gigantischen Türme des World Trade Centers, beträchtlich höher als der Turm der Paulskirche. Beide Türme sind am 11. September 2001 Opfer eines mörderischen Anschlags auf die Vereinigten Staaten von Amerika geworden, und Flugzeuge, normale Verkehrsmaschinen hatten als Waffen gedient, gesteuert von Piloten, die ihre Zerstörung im Sinn hatten um den Preis vieler, vieler Menschenleben. Danach fanden weder die betroffene Stadt noch das angegriffene Land in den alten Rhythmus zurück.

Im Sommer des Jahres 2001 hatte Torsten Andreas Hoffmann New York besucht, um Bilder für einen großformatigen Kalender zu machen. Später, bei der Sichtung des Materials, stellte er fest, dass sich die Zwillingstürme des World Trade Centers häufig in das Blickfeld seiner Kamera geschoben hatten, zu häufig für seine Zwecke. Sein Thema waren nicht die „Twins". Doch nach dem vernichtenden Attentat sind sie es geworden, unvermeidlich beinahe. Wie unter Zwang kehrte der Fotograf an die Stätte des Grauens zurück: Um neue Bilder zu schaffen, andere. Er spürte die Standorte auf, von wo aus er den Blick seiner Kamera auf Nord- und Südturm des World Trade Centers gerichtet hatte, bevor die Flugzeuge zuschlugen. Er rekonstruierte Sicht, Perspektive und Ausschnitt, um die neuen Aufnahmen den früheren gegenüberstellen zu können und so nach ihrem Zusammensturz zu dokumentieren, dass etwas Unvorstellbares geschehen war, indem er zeigt, wie ein Motiv, das kurz zuvor noch wie selbstverständlich anwesend war, plötzlich abwesend ist. Eine beklemmende Leere scheint auf einmal die späteren fotografischen Bilder zu erfüllen.

Bewusst hat der Fotograf auf alle vordergründigen Effekte verzichtet, kein Bild von Ground Zero seiner Auswahl zugefügt, kein Bild von den Aufräumarbeiten, vom (vereinzelten) Bergen der Toten oder ihren Überbleibseln. Keine Wiederholung tausendfach reproduzierter Bilder, die das Fürchterliche bannen und seine Wirkung durch selbstvergessene Wiederholung reduzieren. Stattdessen erwartet er von den Betrachtern seiner

Bilder, dem Unvorstellbaren durch die Tätigkeit ihrer Phantasie Gestalt, Ausmaß und Dauer zu geben, wobei das gezielte Aussparen des Schrecklichen den Prozess der Imagination auslöst und zugleich steuert. Damit eröffnet Hoffmann dem Medium der Fotografie von neuem jene unerschöpflichen Möglichkeiten, die seine Grenzen eigentlich erst bedingen – und die von ihrer Preisgabe an die Kunst nahezu restlos aufgezehrt worden sind: Den Einbruch des Realen in die Bilderwelt zu fixieren und sein gleichzeitiges Verschwinden aus der Erfahrungswelt. Was ein fotografisches Bild zeigt, ist schon im Augenblick der individuellen Wahrnehmung unaufhebbar abwesend, obwohl die Anschauung fortwährend seine (einstige) Anwesenheit beweist. Jede Fotografie bezeugt Vergangenes, dokumentiert sichtbar Anwesendes im Status des faktisch Abwesenden.

Durch eine Verbindung des Vorvergangenen mit dem Vergangenen intensiviert Hoffmann das schmerzliche Gefühl des Verlustes noch und provoziert ein merkwürdiges Gefühlsdilemma. Über der Brooklyn Bridge wölbt sich ein makellos blass blauer Himmel und beherrscht die Hälfte der Bildfläche, wo kurze Zeit zuvor die Zwillingstürme des World Trade Centers aufragten und die Brücke zu einem Ornament zusammenschrumpfen ließen. Der Aufnahmewinkel hat sich leicht verschoben, das aufgeraute tief blaue Wasser erhält im zweiten Bild größeren Spielraum, weil die Proportionen im Bildausschnitt nicht mehr die gleichen sind und um der Bildästhetik willen sachte korrigiert werden mussten – doch mit Ausnahme der fehlenden Türme und dem Umstand, dass heller Tag an Stelle des Morgens oder Abends getreten ist, hat sich nichts verändert. Tatsächlich?

Alles hat sich verändert. Trotz der meisterhaften Führung des Lichts, das im Farbbild die Brücke in ein filigranes Objekt aus Brüsseler Spitze verwandelt und ihr doch die eigenständige Präsenz im Vergleich zur ersten Aufnahme zurückgibt, entsteht der Eindruck, als würde die Leere des Himmels darüber in einer bedrückenden Beredsamkeit schweigen. Je länger man die Aufnahme mustert, desto lastender die Empfindung. Allein deshalb, weil das Bewusstsein, wachgehalten durch die noch gegenwärtige Erinnerung und erneuert durch die zeitlich vorher datierte Aufnahme vis à vis, in der offenen Fläche imaginativ wahrnimmt, was unwiderruflich zu Schutt und Asche wurde, in einem Nachbild sozusagen. Dagegen ist die Erinnerung an die lange Zeit vor Errichtung der mächtigen Türme, die von den New Yorkern damals keineswegs enthusiastisch begrüßt worden sind, fast verloschen.

Andererseits rufen die neuen Bilder auch diese verloschene Erinnerung ins Gedächtnis. Auf eine merkwürdige (und unmögliche) Weise. Ist es nur auf den Farbwechsel zurückzuführen, dass sie erheblich entspannter als die Schwarz-Weiß-Aufnahmen anmuten? Dank der dramatisierenden Eigenschaften der Schwarz-Weiß-Fotografie entfalten die Aufnahmen mit den mitunter schier übermächtigen Zwillingstürmen bisweilen einen spannungsreicheren und – subkutan – auch bedrohlicheren Charakter. Oder tut sich bei der Betrachtung kraft der Gegenüberstellung ein Konflikt zwischen Sehen und Wissen auf? Wissen bestimmt die menschliche Wahrnehmung, und Sehen ist die Folge von unaufhörlich erfahrenen Schocks von ungewohnten Wahrnehmungsimpulsen. Sehen ist ein unaufhörlicher Lernprozess.

St. Pauls Church im Zentrum von „downtown". Passagierflugzeuge fliegen im Minutentakt über Manhattan

St. Pauls Church in downtown. Airplanes fly over Manhattan every minute

Es ist ein seltsames Nachher, dass sich angesichts der extrem hochformatigen oder panoramatischen Bilder, nebeneinander oder übereinander gestellt, einprägt. Verstärkt durch das Bestreben, dass sowohl der fotografische Autor als auch die Einwohner der Stadt den Zustand einer wie auch immer beschaffenen Normalität beschwören. Das Leben geht weiter. Der Gabelstapler in der Henry Street verrichtet nach wie vor sein Tagwerk, und in der nicht abgeflossenen Wasserlache der Straße spiegeln sich wie stets Municipal und Woolworth Building im Zuckerbäckerstil ein paar Blocks nordöstlich des riesigen Trümmerfeldes, vom Desaster verschont – nur die kantigen Wahrzeichen von South Manhattan, die annähernd dreißig Jahre die Silhouette des Distrikts bestimmt hatten, die fehlen; glänzen im schattenlosen Licht des frühen Tages förmlich durch ihre demonstrative Abwesenheit. Vor der beschädigten Silhouette verhalten sich die Menschen an der Uferparade Brooklyns, als sei nichts passiert. Im Battery Park findet sich ein junger Zeitungsleser an Stelle des meditierenden Mannes mit nacktem Oberkörper. Nur von Westen aus gesehen, ist der Einbruch eklatanter. Nahezu verlassen stehen die Gebäude zwei und drei des World Financial Centers ohne ihren gewohnten Rückhalt wie riesige Schachfiguren in der Gegend herum. Sie waren Bestandteil des Ensembles, das sämtliche Dimensionen sprengte.

Torsten Andreas Hoffmann hat mit seiner Kamera die leere Mitte des einstigen Standortes der beiden himmelwärts stürmenden Türme des Welthandelszentrums in New York gleichsam umkreist, hat mit Hilfe seiner Bilder dieser leeren Mitte „sprachlosen" Ausdruck gegeben. Und damit dem Gefühl der Des-Orientierung, das die Menschen der Postmoderne mit wachsender Intensität befällt, eine bestürzende Anschaulichkeit verliehen. Die Hälfte aller Blicke hat sich unversehens in rein fotografische Konstruktionen verwandelt. Ansichten einer fiktiven Wirklichkeit gleichsam. Allein im digitalen Verfahren des Computerbildes werden Nord- und Südturm des World Trade Centers im Süden Manhattans künftig noch so authentisch wie in den zahllosen fotografischen Porträts ihrer Existenz wieder erscheinen können. Als fremd gewordene Vergangenheitsgegenwart.

Klaus Honnef, Bonn, im Dezember 2001

Preface

A mere sliver of silver against a clear sky. The airplane would be invisible if its slender body did not reflect the sunlight. It glides towards the golden weather vane on the steeple of St. Paul's Cathedral in downtown Manhattan – probably passing it at a great distance. Captured on film by photographer Torsten Andreas Hoffmann in the war-pregnant late autumn of 2001. Above a ring of columns and vented windows the steeple of the neo-Baroque church rises peacefully into the sky; a beautiful photograph with wonderful color and formal balance. Yet the terrible memory is there; knowledge and experience that have changed the perception of pictures, especially technical and electronic pictures, in a perhaps lasting, maybe even permanent way.

A few months earlier, the photographer took a photo of the same motif from nearly the same angle also using a strong telephoto lens, but in black and white. An apparently similar photograph, yet totally different. For in this photo the airplane would not have been visible at all, it would have been hidden behind the matrix-like façade of one of the gigantic World Trade Center towers that takes up most the background of the photo, rising high above the steeple of St. Paul's. On September 11, 2001 the twin towers both became victims of a murderous attack on the United States of America and airplanes, normal commercial airplanes, were the weapons used, flown by pilots bent on their destruction at the price of many, many human lives. Afterwards, neither the city nor the country attacked regained their old rhythm.

In the summer of 2001 Torsten Andreas Hoffmann visited New York to take photos for a large format calendar. When examining the photo material later, he determined that the twin towers of the World Trade Center had often pushed themselves in front of his field of vision – too often for his purposes. His topic was not the "twins". Yet after the devastating attack they did become his topic, almost unavoidably. As if under duress, the photographer returned to the scene of horror: to create new images, different images. He went back to the locations from which he had pointed his camera at the north and south towers of the World Trade Center before the airplanes hit. He reconstructed the view, angle and detail in order to be able to compare the new photos to the earlier ones and thus, after the collapse, document that something unfathomable had happened by showing how a motif that shortly before had been present as a matter of course was now suddenly absent. An oppressive absence suddenly seems to fill the later photographic images.

The photographer consciously refrained from using superficial effects: he has not included pictures of Ground Zero, the clean-up work or the (occasional) removal of human remains and the dead. There is no duplication of the pictures reproduced by the thousands that capture the horror and diminish its effect through oblivious repetition. Instead, he expects those viewing his photographs to use their imagination to give the unimaginable form, dimension and duration: the intentional exclusion of the horrific triggers and guides the process of imagination. In doing this, Hoffmann re-opens the medium of

15

Henry Street unterhalb
der Manhattan Bridge

Henry Street under the
Manhattan Bridge

photography to those inexhaustible possibilities that actually define its limits – and which, through their abandonment to Art, have become almost totally depleted: to fixate the incursion of reality into the world of images and simultaneously its disappearance out of the world of experience. That, which a photographic image shows, is already irrevocably absent at the moment of individual perception, although experience continues to prove its (onetime) presence. Each photograph testifies to the past, documents that which is visually present in the status of the factually absent.

In connecting the past with an even earlier past Hoffmann intensifies the painful feeling of loss and provokes a strange affective dilemma. An unblemished light blue sky unfolds above Brooklyn Bridge, dominating half of the photo, where a short time before the twin towers of the World Trade Center soared, turning the bridge into a small ornament. The angle at which the photo was taken has slightly shifted, the rippled, deep blue water is given more room in the second photo, since the proportions in the cropped photo are no longer the same and had to be gently corrected for the sake of aesthetics. Yet with the exceptions of the missing towers and the fact that bright daylight has replaced dawn or dusk, nothing has changed. Really?

Everything has changed. Despite the masterful use of light – which in the color photo turns the bridge into a piece of filigree Brussels lace, restoring its independent presence in comparison to the first photo – it seems as if the emptiness of the sky remains silent with oppressive eloquence. The longer you examine the photograph, the more burdensome this feeling becomes. If only because consciousness, kept alive by memories still present and renewed by the temporally earlier photograph next to it, imaginatively perceives that which has been turned to dust and rubble in the open sky, in a so-called afterimage. In comparison, memories of the long period of time that preceded the erection of the mighty towers, which were by no means enthusiastically welcomed by New Yorkers, have almost died.

Yet on the other hand, the new photos also bring these dead memories to mind. In a strange (and impossible) manner. Is the use of color solely responsible for the fact that the new photos seem considerably more relaxed than the black and white images? Due to the dramatizing characteristics of black and white photography, the photos of the often almost overpowering twin towers sometimes develop a more suspenseful and – subcutaneously – also more threatening character. Or, by virtue of the comparison does a conflict arise during the viewing process between seeing and knowing? Knowledge determines human perception and seeing is the result of the incessantly experienced shock of unfamiliar perceptive stimuli. Seeing is a never-ending learning process.

It is a strange "afterworld" that commits itself to memory in view of the extremely elongated upright format and panorama images set next to or above and below each other. Reinforced by the endeavor of the photographic author as well as the city's inhabitants to conjure up images of some kind of normalcy in this situation. Life goes on. The fork-lift on Henry Street still goes about its work and water still puddles on the street, reflecting as always the wedding-cake styled Municipal and Woolworth Buildings a few blocks northeast of the huge rubble field, untouched by the disaster – only the angular symbols of South Manhattan that characterized the district's skyline for almost 30 years are missing. They are positively conspicuous in the shadowless light of the early morning in their demonstrative absence. In front of the damaged skyline, men on the Brooklyn Promenade behave as if nothing had happened. In Battery Park a young man reading a newspaper occupies the place of the shirtless man meditating. Only when seen from the west is the difference more striking. Nearly deserted, Buildings 2 and 3 of the World Financial Center stand alone like gigantic chess figures without their normal support. They were part of an ensemble that burst all dimensions.

Torsten Andreas Hoffmann circled the empty core where the soaring towers of the World Trade Center in New York once stood and with his photographs has given "speechless" expression to this emptiness; thus lending alarming clarity to the feeling of disorientation, which overcomes postmodern man with increasing intensity. Half of all the views have suddenly been transformed into purely photographic constructions. Images of a fictitious reality, so to speak. In the future, only digitalized computer images will make the North and South towers of the World Trade Center in southern Manhattan appear as authentic as in the countless photographic portraits of their existence. As an estranged past-present.

Klaus Honnef, Bonn, December 2001

Blick von Brooklyn über das Ufer des East River

View from Brooklyn to the bank of the East River

Blick vom Empire State
Building Richtung
Süden

View from Empire State
Building to the south

Brooklyn Bridge

Battery Park

Blick von der Harbor-
side, New Jersey

View from Harborside,
New Jersey

West Street

Woolworth Building

34

Sullivan Street/
Houston Street

Wall Street und Trinity
Church

Wall Street and Trinity
Church

Blick von der Brooklyn Bridge auf Pace University und Woolworth Building

View from the Brooklyn Bridge to Pace University and Woolworth Building

Blick auf die Westseite
des World Financial
Centers von einer
Fähre nach New Jersey

View from a New
Jersey ferry to the west
side of the World
Financial Center

Blick von Brooklyn
über den East River

View from Brooklyn
over the East River

Blick von Brooklyn auf
die Skyline mit Brooklyn
Bridge

Skyline with Brooklyn
Bridge from Brooklyn

Blick von der Williams-
burgh Bridge auf Lower
East Side

Lower East Side from
the Williamsburgh
Bridge

East River, Brooklyn
Bridge

50

Blick von einer Fähre
nach New Jersey

View from a New
Jersey ferry

Monroe Street/Market
Street

Broadway/Fulton Street

Laden am Broadway
gegenüber von
Ground Zero

Shop on the Broadway
vis-à-vis from Ground
Zero

Blick von der
Brooklyn Bridge

View from the
Brooklyn Bridge

Blick von einer Fähre
nach Staten Island

View from a Staten
Island ferry

Blick vom Dach eines
Bürogebäudes in der
44sten Straße

View from the top of
a building in the 44th
Street

Houston Street/West Broadway

Blick vom East Broadway auf Municipal und Woolworth Building

View from East Broadway to Municipal and Woolworth Building

East Broadway, China
Town

Green Street, SoHo

Greenwich Street nähe
Battery Place

Greenwich Steet near
Battery Place

Aussichtspunkt im
Battery Park

Vantage point in
the Battery Park

Busenskulptur im
Battery Park

Breastsculpture in
the Battery Park

Allen Street/Division
Street, Chinatown

Harborside, New Jersey

Skyline vom Ufer aus
Brooklyn

Skyline from the bank
of Brooklyn

Brooklyn Bridge

West Street am Ufer des
Hudson River

West Street at the bank
of the Hudson River

Über den Dächern der
Lower East Side

Over the roofs of the
Lower East Side

East Broadway,
Manhattan Bridge,
Woolworth Building,
Municipal Building

Auf Seite 92 spiegeln
sich die Strukturen des
World Trade Centers in
den Fenstern des World
Financial Centers

On page 92 you can
see the structure of the
World Trade Center in
the windows of the
World Financial Center

Skyline, Brooklyn Bridge

West Street

Blick von einer Staten
Island Fähre

View from a Staten
Island Ferry

Wallstreet

Friseur in der 28. Straße

Hairdresser's shop in
the 28th Street

World Financial Center,
beim Einsturz der Türme
des World Trade Centers
wurden viele weitere
Gebäude beschädigt

World Financial Center,
many other buildings
are damaged by the
falling-in of the World
Trade Center

oben:
Blick auf die Skyline
von Midtown

unten:
Blick von Brooklyn auf
die „beschädigte"
Skyline von „down-
town"

above:
View to the Midtown
Skyline

below:
View from Brooklyn to
the "damaged" skyline
of downtown

Liberty Island mit
Freiheitsstatue

Liberty Island with
the Statue of Liberty

Torsten Andreas Hoffmann, 1956 in Düsseldorf geboren, studierte von 1977–83 Kunstpädagogik mit Schwerpunkt Fotografie bei Michael Ruetz. Seit 1988 arbeitet er als freischaffender Fotograf und Didaktiker (u.a. Lehrauftrag UNI Hildesheim).

Fotoreisen haben ihn u.a. nach Indien, Nepal, Italien, Frankreich, in die Türkei, die USA und die Sahara geführt. Seine Fotografien wurden in zahlreichen Ausstellungen gezeigt (z.B. Expo 2000) und in Buchpublikationen verwendet (z.B. „Workshop kreative Schwarzweiss-Fotografie", Verlag Photographie 2001). Es erschienen Portfolios und Zeitschriftenveröffentlichungen (z.B. in Geo-Saison, Merian, Chrismon, Gestaltungsserie Leica-Fotografie International, SCHWARZWEISS 31). Im Kunstverlag Weingarten erscheinen von ihm grossformatige Fotokunstkalender über New York und Berlin.

In New York hat er einen großen Teil seiner mehrfach ausgestellten Serie „Mensch und Raum" fotografiert. In dieser Serie stellt er die Frage nach dem Verhältnis des modernen Menschen zu seiner Umgebung.

Neben seiner Fotoarbeit leitet Torsten Andreas Hoffmann auch Workshops (u.a. in der imago fotokunst Galerie Berlin), in denen er Interessierten die Gesetzmässigkeiten guter Bildgestaltung vermittelt.

Teile seiner Arbeit sind im Internet unter www.t-a-hoffmann.de zu sehen.

Torsten Andreas Hoffmann, born 1956 in Dusseldorf, studied art education and photography under Michael Ruetz from 1977–1983. Since 1988 he has worked as a freelance photographer and educator (teaching at the University of Hildesheim, among other institutions).

Photography has taken him on trips to many places, including India, Nepal, Italy, France, Turkey, the United States and the Sahara Desert. His photographs have been shown in numerous exhibits (for example, Expo 2000) and used in many publications (including "Workshop kreative Schwarzweiss-Fotografie" (Workshop Creative Black & White photography). Portfolios and magazine publications have appeared in Geo-Saison, Merian, Chrismon, Gestaltungsserie Leica-Fotografie International (Leica Photography International Design Series), SCHWARZWEISS 31 (BLACK & WHITE 31), to name a few. Kunstverlag Weingarten has published his work in large-format calendars on New York and Berlin.

Hoffmann took most of the photographs in his frequently exhibited series "Mensch und Raum" (Man and Space) in New York. This series poses the question as to the relationship of modern man to his environment.

In addition to his photography, Torsten Andreas Hoffmann also leads workshops, for example at Imago Fotokunst Gallery in Berlin, in which he presents the basic laws of good composition.

Some of his work can be seen at www.t-a-hoffmann.de.

TItelabbildung/Cover:
Brooklyn Bridge

Abbildung auf der Rückseite/Back Cover:
Blick vom World Trade Center Richtung Osten auf den East River
und Brooklyn
View from World Trade Center to the East River and Brooklyn in
the east

Die Deutsche Bibliothek – CIP-Einheitshaufnahme
Ein Titeldatensatz für diese Publikation ist bei
Der Deutschen Bibliothek erhältlich

Die Deutsche Bibliothek – CIP Cataloguing-in-Publication-Data
A catalogue record for this publication is available from Die
Deutsche Bibliothek

© 2002 by Kunstverlag Weingarten GmbH, Weingarten
Vorwort/Preface: Klaus Honnef
Übersetzung/Translation: Lynn Hattery-Beyer
Satz/Typesetting: Riedmayer GmbH, Weingarten
Reproduktionen/Reproductions: Repro-Team GmbH, Weingarten
Gesamtherstellung/Printing and Binding: Kösel GmbH & Co. KG,
Kempten
Printed in Germany
ISBN 3-8170-2536-X